THE EXTRAORDINARY LIFE OF MALALA YOUSAFZAI

HIBA NOOR KHAN

LEVEL
2

ADAPTED BY HANNAH FISH
ILLUSTRATED BY RITA PETRUCCIOLI
SERIES EDITOR: SORREL PITTS

PENGUIN BOOKS

UK | USA | Canada | Ireland | Australia
India | New Zealand | South Africa

Penguin Books is part of the Penguin Random House group of companies
whose addresses can be found at global.penguinrandomhouse.com.

www.penguin.co.uk www.puffin.co.uk www.ladybird.co.uk

Penguin
Random House
UK

The Extraordinary Life of Malala Yousafzai first published by Puffin Books, 2019
This Penguin Readers edition published by Penguin Books Ltd, 2020

001

Original text written by Hiba Noor Khan
Text for Penguin Readers edition adapted by Hannah Fish
Text copyright © Hiba Noor Khan, 2019
Illustrated by Rita Petruccioli
Illustrations copyright © Rita Petruccioli, 2019 and 2020
Cover image by Rita Petruccioli

The moral right of the original author and the original illustrator has been asserted.

Printed and bound in Great Britain by Clays Ltd, Elcograf S.p.A.

A CIP catalogue record for this book is available from the British Library

ISBN: 978-0-241-44737-6

All correspondence to
Penguin Books
Penguin Random House Children's Books
One Embassy Gardens, New Union Square
5 Nine Elms Lane, Londong SW8 5DA

MIX
Paper from
responsible sources
FSC® C018179
www.fsc.org

Penguin Random House is committed to a
sustainable future for our business, our readers
and our planet. This book is made from Forest
Stewardship Council® certified paper.

Contents

People in the book

Malala Yousafzai

Malala's father, Ziauddin

Malala's mother, Toor Pekai

Malala with her brothers, Atal and Khushal

New words

army

attack

journalist

prize

religion

valley

war

Note about the book

Malala Yousafzai lived in Pakistan. Pakistan is an **Islamic***
country. **Islam** is a very important religion across the
world and the **Quran** is the book of the Islamic religion.
The Taliban are a group of Islamist **extremists**. The
Taliban started in 1994 in Afghanistan – a country next
to Pakistan.

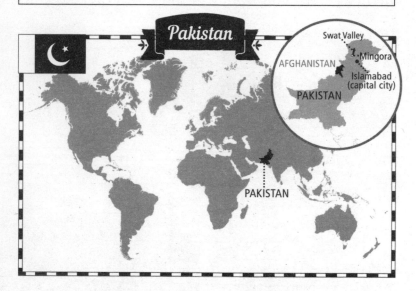

Before-reading questions

1 What do you know about Malala Yousafzai?
2 What do you know about Pakistan and the Taliban?
3 Read the back cover of the book. What more do you
know now?
4 What information would you like to find out from
this book?

*Definitions of words in **bold** can be found in the glossary on pages 62–63.

CHAPTER ONE
Who is Malala Yousafzai?

Malala Yousafzai **was born** on 12th July 1997 in the beautiful Swat Valley in the north of Pakistan.

Malala's father was a teacher and he and Malala's mother always wanted her to do very well at school. Malala loved learning about everything, and she was always one of the best students in her class.

Malala was a very happy little girl. She often played with her friends and her two younger brothers in the green Swat Valley.

But then a group of **Islamist extremists** called the Taliban came from Afghanistan to Malala's valley and a war began. After this, everything changed.

The Taliban wanted to stop girls going to school and this made Malala and her father very angry. They thought that this was very **unfair** and spoke about it to many people. Malala was very **brave**. She did not stop going to school, but every day she went there **in secret**.

A Taliban soldier

After some time, the Pakistan army fought the Taliban. The Taliban left Malala's town and Malala and the other girls of the Swat Valley could go to school again.

Many people around the world heard about Malala and the Taliban. "Girls must be able to go to school," Malala always said.

Then one day, two men from the Taliban **shot** Malala on the bus home from school.

Malala was in hospital for a very long time, but after this she **became** famous across the world. She was a very brave and kind young girl, and she later got the **Nobel Peace Prize**.

But let's go back to the start and little Malala in the Swat Valley . . .

CHAPTER TWO
Malala in the Swat Valley

The Swat Valley is very beautiful and many people visit this part of Pakistan every year. For a long time Malala's family were poor, but they lived in a wonderful place. Near their little village there were clean rivers, green trees, tall **mountains** and beautiful bright colours. Malala often tells people, "We lived in the most beautiful place in all the world!"

Malala's grandfather studied in India and then became a teacher. He learned from watching and listening to many great people. Two of the most important people at that time were Mahatma Ghandi from India and Muhammad Ali Jinnah from Pakistan.

Mahatma Ghandi

Malala's grandfather was an intelligent man and her father always worked very hard to make his father happy.

Malala's father's name is Ziauddin Yousafzai. School was very difficult for Ziauddin. The other children at school laughed at him because he was darker and shorter than they were. Ziauddin also had problems speaking. Sometimes he stopped and started his sentences and it was difficult for him to get his words out.

But Ziauddin worked very hard at school because he really wanted to make his father happy. He learned how to be strong, and he became a very kind and intelligent man.

Ziauddin Yousafzai

Malala's mother's name is Toor Pekai, and she only went to school for a short time. This was normal for girls in the Swat Valley at that time. Toor Pekai's father wanted her to go to school, but she was the only girl in her class. She did not feel happy about this.

Toor Pekai

Malala's parents met, and they married about nine months later. Ziauddin really wanted to open his own school and Toor Pekai wanted to help him. "Pakistan has many problems," Ziauddin said to his wife. "But the answer to these problems is for children to go to school. We can help. We can open a school."

It took many years and a lot of hard work for Ziauddin to open his school, and he gave it the name the Khushal School. The school was in Mingora, a town in the Swat Valley. Later, Toor Pekai started working at the school, too.

Toor Pekai was very happy to live in a bigger place with more people, but it was not easy. It was very difficult to pay for the school and for food. One year there was a bad **flood** at the school. This was a very difficult time for the Khushal School and for Malala's parents. But their love was strong, and they worked together to keep the school open.

The Kushal School

Malala was born on 12th July 1997. Ziauddin loved his daughter, and he wrote and sang songs about her. His school now had about 100 students and six teachers. Malala and her parents lived above the school, and little Malala played in the classrooms.

Baby Malala

The family were poor at this time, but in the next two or three years, more and more students came to the school and things got easier. After some time, they had more money. Now they could open a new school. They gave this school the name the Malala Education Academy.

Malala's first baby brother, Khushal, was born in 1999. Malala was two years old then. Five years later, her other baby brother, Atal, was born. Malala's family was small – many families from the Swat Valley had seven or eight children.

Malala with Atal and Khushal

The family bought a new house and Ziauddin's friends often visited in the evenings. They sat with him to drink tea and to talk about many things. Malala was an intelligent girl and always enjoyed sitting with them and listening to them.

The family's new home was in a part of Mingora called Gulkada or Butkara. Malala loved looking at the beautiful mountains near their town. The tallest mountain was called Mount Elum, and the top of this mountain was high up in the sky.

Malala was a happy little girl and she loved her father very much. Sometimes she was sad or angry, but talking to her father always helped.

Malala with her father, Ziauddin

The family often went back to Malala's grandparents' village for special days, and they enjoyed doing this. They wore their best clothes and brought sweets and other nice things. Malala and her brothers always wanted to sit next to the windows on the bus. They drove through the valley and looked out of the windows at the beautiful mountains, rivers and trees.

But not everything was good in the Swat Valley. Everyone had to leave their **rubbish** in the valley because there was no one to take it away. The rubbish grew into an ugly mountain and Malala did not like going there with her family's rubbish. One day, she saw someone on the big rubbish mountain. It was a very poor girl with very dirty hair. The girl looked through the rubbish and put some of it into a big bag. At that time, many children took **metal** from the rubbish mountain for money. This made Malala very sad.

Malala really wanted to help people and to make them happy. And first, she wanted to help the children on the rubbish mountain.

CHAPTER THREE

The war begins

On 11th September 2001, Malala was only four years old. Across the world in New York City in the United States of America (USA), a **terrible** thing happened. The Islamist **extremist** group al-Qaeda flew two planes into the World Trade Center and killed thousands of people.

Many people from al-Qaeda were in Afghanistan at that time. People in the USA were very angry about the attacks on the World Trade Center, and their army **bombed** many places in Afghanistan. Thousands more people were killed. Malala was too young to understand, but war was now close to her quiet valley.

Afghanistan was the home of the Islamist extremist group, the Taliban. The Taliban were now also in some parts of Pakistan, near to Afghanistan. The people of the Swat Valley did not like the extremists, but they were also very angry about the **American bombs** in Afghanistan. In 2004, many people in Pakistan **supported** the Taliban, and the USA bombed Pakistan for the first time.

Afghanistan was the home of the Taliban.

The people of Pakistan had the extremists on one side and the American bombs on the other. Malala's father and his friends met with 150 people from the Swat Valley. They talked about stopping the fighting.

Then the Taliban came to the Swat Valley. "Poor people need help and the Taliban can help them," they said. In 2005, there was a terrible **earthquake** and many people died. Lots of people had no houses to live in, and it was difficult to get food and water to people. The Taliban helped a lot of people after the earthquake.

But the Taliban wanted women and girls to stay at home and not to go to school. On the radio, they told people, "It says this in the **Quran**." The Taliban used the radio because not many people had a television at that time.

The Taliban spoke on the radio.

"Don't listen to the Taliban," Ziauddin told his family. "The religion of **Islam** does not stop girls going to school."

But many people started to listen to the Taliban. Some of the teachers at Ziauddin's schools stopped teaching girls. Lots of girls stopped going to their classes because they were frightened of the Taliban. But Malala put her school clothes and school books in her bag, walked with her head down, and went to school in secret.

Malala went to school in secret.

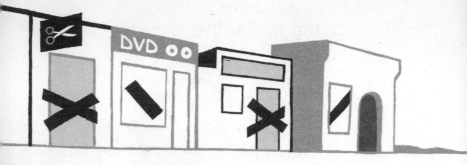

The Taliban closed many shops.

Things became worse. The Taliban closed many shops. They sent men out on to the streets. The men had to watch people and tell them what to do. These men stopped people doing normal things. The Taliban were **dangerous**.

Then things became really bad – the Taliban started to attack the Swat Valley. Malala's quiet and beautiful home quickly became a dark and dangerous place of war for the Taliban and the **Americans**.

CHAPTER FOUR

Living under the Taliban

The Taliban were in the Swat Valley and things were very bad for the people there. Children could not play many games or watch many things on television. People could not do normal things, and living with the extremists was very difficult.

The Taliban spoke about their religion, but it was different to the people's Islam. The people did not know this religion. The beautiful Swat Valley was not the same.

The war quickly moved to other parts of Pakistan and to the capital city, Islamabad. Many people died and the country had terrible problems.

The Pakistan army arrived in the Swat Valley and they looked for the Taliban. The men from the army flew over the valley and they threw sweets and balls to the children.

Malala was now in the top class at a new school. She worked very hard, and she and her best friend, Moniba, were very good students. The days of war were very dark, but school gave Malala and Moniba a place to laugh and to forget about the problems of the world. They enjoyed working together and writing funny stories.

At school, Malala could forget about the problems of the world.

But in the streets, the bombs did not stop falling. Sometimes they hit the ground very close to Malala's home. This made her and her brothers very frightened.

Malala's father and his friends wanted to tell people about the war and about the Taliban. They started speaking to journalists about the war and the problems in Pakistan.

Malala also wanted to talk to journalists. In 2008, she spoke to a big group of people about the Taliban. "They are very dangerous," she said. She was only eleven years old.

Every day things got worse and worse. The Taliban did not speak about the true **Islamic** religion. Now they wanted to stop *all* girls going to school. The people of the Swat Valley did not support the Taliban now, but they did not try to fight them because they were too frightened.

Many children did not play normal games — they played 'Army and Taliban' games. It was difficult to sleep at night because the noise from the bombs was very loud. Malala and her brothers often woke up in the night and were very frightened.

Malala often woke up in the night.

Malala did not stop talking to journalists about the war. Then the **BBC** asked her to write about living in the Swat Valley with the Taliban. At the start, she used a different name and she emailed her work to a journalist in secret. Then he emailed it to the BBC.

Malala wanted to tell her story – it was important. In the next few months, many people across the world read about Malala.

In 2008, a very dark day came for Malala. The Taliban stopped girls going to school. This made Malala and her friends very sad, and on her last day of school, Malala cried and cried.

Malala told the world her story. She wanted people to know about the problems in Pakistan. "Don't tell your story," many people told her. "The Taliban are dangerous men." But Malala was very brave, and she did not stop speaking.

A few months later, the fighting in Mingora got worse. The Pakistan army wanted everyone in the town to leave. Then they could fight the Taliban and get them out of Pakistan. Malala's family were very sad to leave. The Swat Valley was their home, and they loved it very much.

Malala and her family had to leave Mingora.

CHAPTER FIVE
Going home

Malala's family left Mingora, and they lived in four different towns in two months. Malala had her twelfth birthday on 12th July, but nobody remembered it. It was very different from her eleventh birthday one year before – at home with her friends and family, and a big birthday cake!

Malala's family lived in four different towns in two months.

After many months, the fighting in Mingora was finished. Now Malala and her family could go home. They drove through the streets of their city, but the streets were not the same.

Everything was different because of the bombs. Many of the buildings had no walls. There were no houses, schools or shops – only mountains of **bricks** and metal.

The streets were not the same.

All the people of Mingora worked together to clean the town, and after some time the school opened again. This was the most wonderful news for the children of Mingora, and many cried because they were very happy. The children met their friends again, and they smiled, laughed and played together.

The Pakistan army were everywhere.

But the Pakistan army were everywhere. The Taliban were not in the town now, but many of them were in the mountains. And the mountains were very close to the Swat Valley. People in Mingora were frightened of the Taliban.

In Mingora, the shops opened, and women and girls walked on the streets again. But things were not the same as before. The war killed many people. A lot of people and their families and friends died in the fighting. Mingora was very different now.

The Swat Valley looked different now, too. Lots of the trees died, and in 2010 there was a terrible flood. Trees can stop a flood, but now there were not many trees in the valley. The flood killed thousands of people. It was difficult for Malala and her family, and for many other people, to get food to cat.

Then the Taliban came back to the Swat Valley. There were attacks on two schools, and they killed some of Malala's father's friends.

**A flood in the Swat Valley
killed thousands of people.**

CHAPTER SIX
Malala speaks to the world

Malala's story for the BBC was now famous across the world. Every day people asked her to speak on the television or on the radio and tell her story. People across the world supported her and wanted to help her. She got a lot of prizes for being very brave and speaking about the Taliban.

Many schools in Pakistan now had "Malala" in their names. Malala also got Pakistan's National Youth Peace Prize, and this prize came with a lot of money.

Malala helped other people with this money. She gave it to street children – children with no houses to live in – and to schools.

Malala got Pakistan's National Youth Peace Prize.

Malala spoke in many different cities. She enjoyed being famous, but she did not forget the most important thing – girls all across the world must go to school and learn. She wanted school to be the same for girls and boys. Malala did not want to stop speaking until this happened.

The people of Pakistan knew and loved Malala and her father. Everyone knew their story and they supported them. They did not support the Taliban now. The religion of the Taliban was not the religion of Pakistan. But the extremist group knew about Malala and her father, too.

Malala and her father on television.

Malala was nearly fifteen years old now. One day, the Taliban put a video on the internet – they wanted to kill Malala. Ziauddin and Toor Pekai were very frightened, but Malala was brave. She did not want to stop fighting for girls to go to school. It was very important to her.

In October 2012, it was time for **exams** at Khushal School and Malala worked very hard. The night before her first exam, Malala studied hard and went to bed very late.

One afternoon that week, Malala got on the school bus to go home with her friends. It was a hot day, and they talked about the exam questions. Then Malala and her friends saw two young men, and everything changed.

"Which girl is Malala?" the men asked. Then they shot her in the head. An ambulance took her to hospital, but things were very bad for Malala.

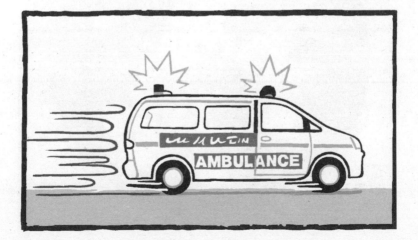

In the next few days, doctors worked very hard. They had to help Malala quickly. They moved her to a big hospital in Peshawar, in Pakistan. After a very long **operation**, the doctors were happy. Malala did not die. But she was not well and the doctors moved her again, to a hospital in Birmingham, England.

BIRMINGHAM

Later, Malala's family flew to England, too. They wanted to be with her at this very important and difficult time.

After three months, Malala left the hospital in Birmingham, but she could not see, hear, smile or walk very well. It took many more months for Malala to do these things again.

CHAPTER SEVEN

Living in England

Malala's family now lived in Birmingham, in England, but they never stopped fighting the Taliban. At her new school, Malala worked very hard and she was one of the best students in her class.

People across the world sent cards and letters to Malala. They were very sad about the attack and wanted Malala to get well quickly.

On her sixteenth birthday, Malala spoke at the United Nations in New York. To people across the world, Malala said, "One child, one teacher, one book and one pen can change the world."

Malala's family travelled to New York with her. Her younger brother, Atal, asked her, "Why are you famous?" He was more interested in seeing famous places in New York than listening to Malala speak!

"One child, one teacher, one book and one pen can change the world."

The Taliban wanted to stop Malala, but they could not. Their attack on Malala made her more famous. Now people across the world understood and supported this brave young woman.

Malala got the Nobel Peace Prize in 2014. She is the youngest person to get this prize. Malala used the $500,000 prize money to help other girls across the world to go to school.

Malala got the Nobel Peace Prize in 2014.

Every year, on her birthday, Malala goes to meet and work with girls in different countries. These girls have many different problems and Malala tries to help them and support them. On her seventeenth birthday she was with girls in Nigeria. On her eighteenth birthday she helped girls in Syria. And on her nineteenth birthday she was with girls in Rwanda and Kenya.

Malala in Rwanda.

After school, Malala studied at the University of Oxford in England. She worked hard at university and today Malala is working hard for girls across the world.

Malala at Oxford University.

During-reading questions

Write the answers to these questions in your notebook.

CHAPTER ONE

1 Where was Malala Yousafzai born?
2 How many brothers does Malala have?
3 Why did a war begin in the Swat Valley?
4 Why did Malala go to school in secret?
5 Why did the Taliban leave the Swat Valley?
6 What happened to Malala on the school bus?

CHAPTER TWO

1 What are the names of Malala's parents?
2 Why did Malala's mother not stay at school?
3 Why did Ziauddin want to open a school?
4 Where was Ziauddin's first school?
5 When was Malala born?
6 What did Malala see at the rubbish mountain?

CHAPTER THREE

1 What happened on 11th September 2001?
2 What did the American army do?
3 Why did the people of the Swat Valley need help?
4 Why did some teachers stop teaching girls?

CHAPTER FOUR

1 Why was school a good place for Malala?
2 Who did Malala and her father speak to about the war?
3 Why did Malala and her brothers often wake up in the night?
4 Who asked Malala to write about living in the Swat Valley with the Taliban?
5 Why did Malala and her family leave the Swat Valley?

CHAPTER FIVE

1 Who cleaned Mingora after the war?
2 Why were the children of Mingora happy?
3 Where were many of the Taliban now?
4 The Taliban came back to the Swat Valley. Who did they kill?

CHAPTER SIX

1 Why did Malala get a lot of prizes?
2 What did Malala do with the money from the National Youth Peace Prize?
3 Why did Malala go to hospital in an ambulance?
4 How long was Malala in hospital in Birmingham for?

CHAPTER SEVEN

1 What did Malala do on her sixteenth birthday?
2 What did Malala get in 2014?
3 What does Malala do on her birthday every year?

After-reading questions

1 Why did the Taliban make Malala and her father angry?
2 How did the Swat Valley change because of the war?
3 Why did two men from the Taliban shoot Malala?
4 What do you think about Malala and her father?
5 What do you think about Malala's story?

Exercises

1 **Match the words with their definitions in your notebook.**

Example: *1 – b*

1	extremists	**a**	not frightened
2	unfair	**b**	These people have very strong ideas.
3	brave	**c**	to hurt or kill someone with a gun
4	in secret	**d**	nobody knows about it
5	shoot	**e**	not right, because not everyone can have the same thing

2 **Are these sentences *true* or *false*? Write the correct answers in your notebook.**

1 School was very difficult for Malala's father. ...*true*...
2 Malala's mother did not stay at school.
3 There was a flood at the Malala Education Academy.
4 Malala and her family lived in Mingora.
5 Malala did not like going to her grandparents' village.

3 **Write the correct adjective in your notebook.**

1 On 11th September 2001, a **brave** / *terrible* thing happened.
2 People in Pakistan were **angry** / **unfair** about the American bombs in Afghanistan.
3 There was an earthquake and it was **difficult** / **easy** to get food and water to people.
4 Many people were **frightened** / **happy** of the Taliban.
5 Things were very **bad** / **quiet** in the Swat Valley.

CHAPTER FOUR

Complete these sentences in your notebook, using the words from the box.

| secret | religion | stories | army | girls | bombs |

1 The Taliban spoke about _religion_, but it was different to the people's Islam.
2 The Pakistan .... arrived in the Swat Valley and they looked for the Taliban.
3 Malala and her best friend, Moniba, wrote ....
4 Sometimes .... hit the ground very close to Malala's home.
5 Malala sent her work to the BBC in ....
6 The Taliban stopped all .... going to school.

5 Look at the picture on page 35, and answer the questions in your notebook.
1 Who are they?   2 When is this?
3 Why are they crying?

CHAPTER FIVE

6 Complete the sentences in your notebook with the past simple form of the verb.
1 Malala's family _lived_ (**live**) in four different towns in two months.
2 After the war, Malala's school .... (**open**) again.
3 The Taliban .... (**wait**) in the mountains close to the Swat Valley.
4 Things in Mingora .... (**are**) not the same as before.
5 Many trees in the valley .... (**die**) because of the war.
6 The Taliban .... (**come**) back to the Swat Valley.

CHAPTER SIX

7 **Correct these sentences in your notebook.**

1 Malala got a lot of books for being brave.
   *Example: Malala got a lot of **prizes** for being brave.*

2 Many schools in Pakistan now had "Ziauddin" in their names.

3 The religion of the Taliban was the same as the religion of Pakistan.

4 The Taliban put a video on the internet – they wanted to help Malala.

5 The night before her first exam, Malala went to bed early.

6 The doctors moved Malala to a hospital in London, in England.

CHAPTER SEVEN

8 **Write short answers to these questions in your notebook.**

1 Did Malala's family live in Birmingham now? *Yes, they did.*

2 Did Malala speak at the United Nations in New York?

3 Was Atal interested in listening to Malala?

4 Could the Taliban stop Malala?

5 Did Malala study at the University of Cambridge?

Project work

1 Imagine you are Malala Yousafzai. Think about your time in the Swat Valley with the Taliban. Write a one-week diary of that time.

2 In this book, you read about Pakistan. Find out more about the country. Make a poster about it. Draw some pictures for your poster.

3 In this book, you read about Malala's story. Find out about Malala today.
   • Where does she live?
   • What job does she do?
   • How old is she this year? What did she do on her birthday?
   • Does she help other people? How does she help them?

4 Write about this book. Did you like it? Did you like the people in it? Why/Why not?

5 Go online and read about Birmingham, England. Then, write a letter from Malala to her friend Moniba. In your letter, tell Moniba about living in Birmingham. Tell her about the place, the people and the food.

6 Draw pictures of these people from the book. Then write two sentences about each person to go with their picture.
   Malala   Ziauddin   Toor Pekai

7 What do you think of this sentence? Why?
'One child, one teacher, one book and one pen can change the world.'

Glossary

American (adj. and n.)
An *American* is someone from
the United States of America.
Something is *American* when it
comes from the United States
of America.

BBC (n.)
(= British Broadcasting
Corporation) The BBC makes
TV and radio.

be born (v.)
A baby comes out from its
mother's body. It *is born*.

become (past simple: *became*) (v.)
to start to be something

bomb (v. and n.)
People *bomb* buildings or other
people. *Bombs* come down from
a plane and hit buildings or
people on the ground.

brave (adj.)
A *brave* person is not frightened.

brick (n.)
You build a wall or house with
bricks.

dangerous (adj.)
A *dangerous* thing can hurt you.

earthquake (n.)
In an *earthquake*, the ground
moves. Buildings sometimes fall
down and people die.

exam (n.)
You have *exams* at school.
You write answers to some
questions.

extremist (n. and adj.)
An *extremist* has very strong
ideas. An *extremist* group
sometimes hurts or kills people
because of these ideas.

flood (n.)
In a *flood* a lot of water goes
over land or buildings.

in secret (phr.)
You do something *in secret*,
and no one knows about it.

Islam (n.); **Islamic** (adj.)
Islamic people believe in *Islam*
(= a religion). They learn and
follow Muhammad's ideas.

Islamist (adj.)
believing very strongly in the
ideas and laws of Islam

metal (n.)
We make money, cars, knives,
forks, etc. with *metal*.

mountain (n.)
A *mountain* is very high. People climb *mountains*. You can also make a *mountain* of things. The Swat Valley has a *mountain* of rubbish.

Nobel Peace Prize (n.)
People get the *Nobel Peace Prize* because they try to stop fighting in the world.

operation (n.)
A doctor does an *operation*. The doctor cuts open a person's body and takes something out or makes it better.

Quran (n.)
The *Quran* is a book. It is the most important book for Muslims (= Islamic people).

rubbish (n.)
things you do not want

shoot (past simple: *shot*) (v.)
You *shoot* with a gun because you want to hurt or kill someone.

support (v.)
to try and help someone

terrible (adj.)
very bad

unfair (adj.)
not right, because everyone cannot do or have the same thing

Penguin  Readers

Visit **www.penguinreaders.co.uk**
for FREE Penguin Readers resources
and digital and audio versions of this book.